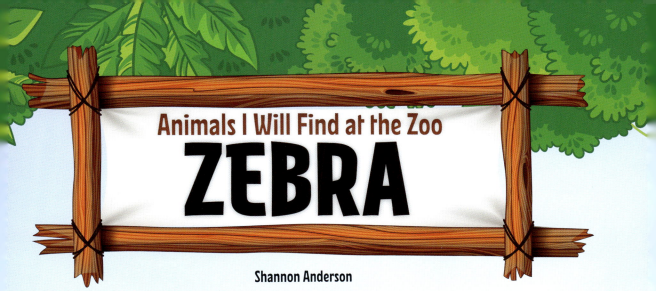

Animals I Will Find at the Zoo
ZEBRA

Shannon Anderson

Table of Contents

ZEBRA	3
WORDS TO KNOW	22
INDEX	23
COMPREHENSION QUESTIONS	23
ABOUT THE AUTHOR	24

A Starfish Book

Teaching Tips for Caregivers:

As a caregiver, you can help your child succeed in school by giving them a strong foundation in language and literacy skills and a desire to learn to read.

This book helps children grow by letting them practice reading skills.

Reading for pleasure and interest will help your child to develop reading skills and will give your child the opportunity to practice these skills in meaningful ways.

- Encourage your child to read on her own at home
- Encourage your child to practice reading aloud
- Encourage activities that require reading
- Establish a reading time
- Talk with your child
- Give your child writing materials

Teaching Tips for Teachers:

Research shows that one of the best ways for students to learn a new topic is to read about it.

Before Reading

- Read the "Words to Know" and discuss the meaning of each word.
- Read the back cover to see what the book is about.

During Reading

- When a student gets to a word that is unknown, ask them to look at the rest of the sentence to find clues to help with the meaning of the unknown word.
- Ask the student to write down any pages of the book that were confusing to them.

After Reading

- Discuss the main idea of the book.
- Ask students to give one detail that they learned in the book by showing a text dependent answer from the book.

ZEBRA

A zoo is a fun place to see animals and learn about them.

One animal you may find in a zoo is a zebra.

Zebras look like striped horses.

But they are smaller than horses.

They have short, stiff **manes**.

Every zebra's stripes are different.

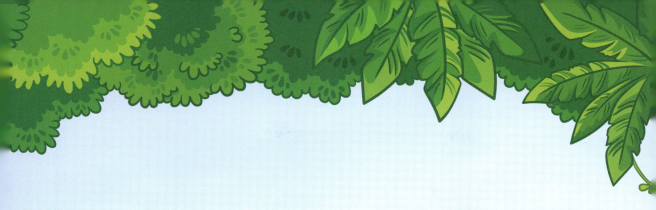

Zebras are **herbivores**.

They graze on grass and other plants for most of the day.

Zebras live in large groups called **herds**.

During the dry season, herds walk a long way to find water and food.

When animal groups move to find food, it is called migration.

Zebras have the longest migration of any land animal.

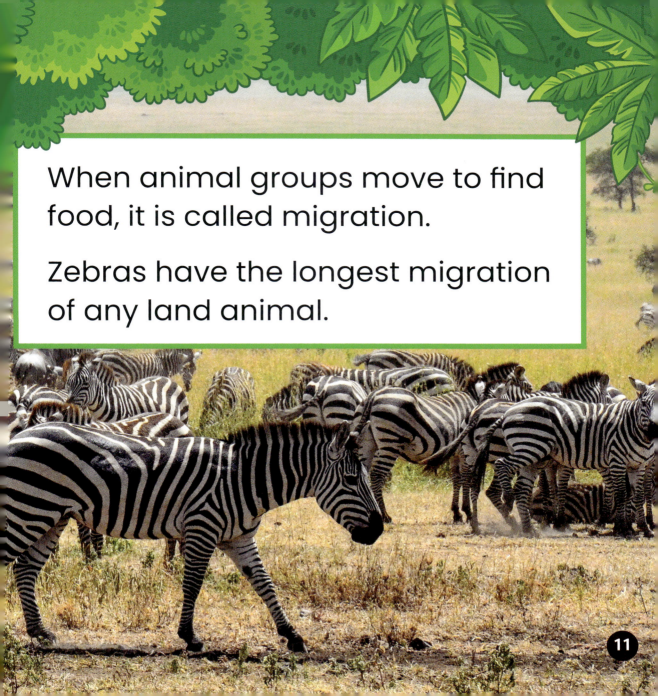

Baby zebras are called foals.

Zebras are **mammals**, so foals drink their mom's milk.

Boy zebras are called stallions, and girl zebras are called mares.

Foals stand and walk less than an hour after they are born.

A mom and her new foal stay away from other zebras for the first few days.

Zebras can run 40 miles (65 kilometers) per hour.

Foals sleep lying down, but adults sleep standing up.

A stallion will stay awake to stand guard while everyone else sleeps.

Strong, healthy zebras can live up to 20 years in the wild.

Most can live up to 30 years in a zoo.

Zebras live in **Africa**.

If you cannot go to Africa to see zebras, you can find them at the zoo!

Words to Know

Africa (AF-ri-kuh): one of Earth's continents; the continent south of the Mediterranean Sea

herbivores (HUR-buh-vors): animals that eat only plants

herds (hurdz): large groups of animals that stay together or move together

mammals (MAM-uhlz): animals that have hair or fur, that give birth to live babies, and that make milk to feed their babies

manes (maynz): growths of thick hair on the heads and necks of lions, horses, zebras, and some other animals

Index

Africa 20, 21
baby/foals 12, 14, 16
graze 7
groups 8, 11
migration 11
sleep 16

Comprehension Questions

1. What are baby zebras called?
   a. colts   b. mares   c. foals

2. What do zebras like to eat?
   a. insects   b. grass   c. berries

3. Male zebras are called ___.
   a. stallions   b. mares   c. foals

4. True or False: Mother zebras take care of their babies.

5. True or False: Adult zebras sleep standing up.

Answers
1. c 2. b 3. a 4. True 5. True

About the Author

Shannon Anderson is an award-winning children's book author and former elementary school teacher. She loves animals and has eight pets of her own. You can learn more about her or invite her to your school at www.shannonisteaching.com.

Written by: Shannon Anderson
Design by: Under the Oaks Media
Editor: Kim Thompson

Library of Congress PCN Data
Zebra / Shannon Anderson
Animals I Will Find at the Zoo
ISBN 979-8-8873-5354-8 (hard cover)
ISBN 979-8-8873-5439-2 (paperback)
ISBN 979-8-8873-5524-5 (EPUB)
ISBN 979-8-8873-5609-9 (eBook)
Library of Congress Control Number: 2022949066

Printed in the United States of America.

Photographs/Shutterstock: Lucian Coman: cover; Andre Anita: p. 3; BlueSnap: p. 5; jmac23: p. 6; Jeff Cable Photography: p. 9; Trek Bears Photography: p. 10; Tomsickova Tatyana: p. 12; Michael Potter11: p. 13; Joanna Rigby-Jones: p. 14; Stu Porter: p. 15; Matsenko Photography: p. 17; sukpaibbonwat: p. 19; Pyty: p. 20(map); Viktor Prymachenko: p. 20; dark side of pink: p. 21

Seahorse Publishing Company
www.seahorsepub.com

Copyright © 2024 **SEAHORSE PUBLISHING COMPANY**

All rights reserved. No part of this publication may be reproduced, stored in a retrieval system or be transmitted in any form or by any means, electronic, mechanical, photocopying, recording, or otherwise, without the prior written permission of Seahorse Publishing Company.

Published in the United States
Seahorse Publishing
PO Box 771325
Coral Springs, FL 33077